W9-ANW-320

ABOUT THIS BOOK

This is a book about horoscopes and the unseen world for the ordinary person. It answers the question, "Is there anything to the claim that some people can read minds and predict the future?" But it also answers a lot of other questions as it surveys psychic phenomena and arcane practices . . . from a witches' coven on Long Island to the Church of Satan in San Francisco . . . from the beginnings of the zodiac five thousand years ago in Mesopotamia to Jeane Dixon's horoscope column in today's *Chicago Tribune* . . . from King Saul's seance with the Witch of Endor to Bishop Pike's session with medium Arthur Ford on the Canadian Television Network . . . from seventeenth-century witch trials in Salem, Massachusetts, to jet-set Sybil Leek's practice of witchcraft in Melbourne Beach, Florida.

Demon possession, voodoo, experiments in extrasensory perception, the strange predictions of Nostradamus 400 years ago: these are some of the subjects considered in this book. A "Glossary of the Occult" will be helpful to many readers. But this book is not a mere collection of information; it examines the life style in contemporary America that may have produced this flowering of interest in the unseen spirit world. This could be its greatest value.

ABOUT THE AUTHOR

Joseph Bayly likes to write about current issues, the things that are exciting people's interest today, the questions they're asking. Last year, in *The View From a Hearse,* he examined the process of dying in our death-denying culture. That book was an immediate success: 36,000 copies were sold in the first six months after publication. This year it's our obsession with the spirit world. "I suddenly woke up to the tremendous influence people like Jeane Dixon and Carroll Righter were having on 40 or 50 million Americans through their daily newspaper columns and articles in the slick magazines. Half the people I met seemed to be following their horoscope. They'd laugh about it, sometimes be a bit apologetic, but you could tell it was on their minds. So I decided to learn everything I could about mediums and witches and the world of the occult." The author combines careful research with willingness to go out on a limb of personal opinion; he is seldom neutral and dispassionate. This makes for interesting reading.

WHAT ABOUT HOROSCOPES?

JOSEPH BAYLY

DAVID C. COOK PUBLISHING CO.
Elgin, Illinois

Quotation from *The Other Side*, by James A. Pike. Copyright © 1968, by New Focus Foundation. Reprinted by Permission of Doubleday & Company, Inc.

Quotation from *Ring of Truth*, by J. B. Phillips, reprinted with permission of The Macmillan Company. Copyright © 1967, by J. B. Phillips.

Quotation from *Hidden Communion, Studies in the Communication Theory of Telepathy* by Dr. Joost A. M. Meerlo, Garret Publications. Copyright © 1964 by Dr. Joost A. M. Meerlo. Used by permission.

WHAT ABOUT HOROSCOPES?

Published for the David C. Cook Publishing Co. by Pyramid Publications

Copyright © 1970 by David C. Cook Publishing Co.

All rights reserved. This book, or parts thereof, may not be reproduced in any form without permission of the publisher, except by a reviewer who wishes to quote brief passages in connection with a review in a magazine or newspaper.

Fourth printing, June 1972

Printed in the United States of America

Library of Congress Catalog Card Number 79-113866

DAVID C. COOK PUBLISHING CO.
Elgin, Illinois 60120

CONTENTS

IS THERE an unseen world, a world our hands cannot touch, our eyes cannot see, our ears cannot hear, a world we cannot taste or smell? And if there is such a world, does it influence life on this planet earth—my life in Yonkers or Springfield or Dallas?

The answer to this question is affirmative from a wide variety of people.

Jeane Dixon says yes, and if you were born under the sign of Cancer (June 22 to July 22), then on September 27 you had better be prepared for trouble: "Sudden changes are quite possible, which seem at this time to be cataclysmic disasters, but which later prove to be the only mechanism by which you can develop."

And because you know that Mrs. Dixon predicted the assassination of President John F. Kennedy in 1963, you listen to her, and just possibly you're a bit more careful driving your car or talking to the boss that day.

Or you read Carroll Righter's horoscope column in the *Chicago Daily News* of Friday, January 16, and—supposing you're a Leo, born between July 23 and August 22—you may decide to kick up your heels a bit that day: "Act in a positive way," Mr. Righter advises you. "Be off to the social with charming people and have a delightful and profitable time."

According to *Editor and Publisher*, 1,200 daily newspapers in the United States publish horoscope columns, compared to only 100 papers 20 years ago.

Business firms employ full-time astrologers. In 1969 Lloyd Cope was retained by New York's Abraham & Straus department store as its official astrology consultant; and a member of the New York Stock Exchange "likes to conclude important deals at three A.M. because of his astrologer's counsel." (*Life* Magazine)

Sybil Leek is a self-proclaimed, practicing witch. Not in seventeenth-century Salem, Massachusetts, but in late twentieth-century Melbourne Beach, Florida, from which she flies (by jet) to New York and Chicago to promote fortune-telling and her new book. Mrs. Leek, who counts 400 "authentic witches" among her personal friends and acquaintances in the United States, estimates the world witch population at eight million.

Other witches (the term "warlock" for a male witch is falling into disuse) include an Air Force captain who has his degree in physics from Virginia Military Institute; a British Ph.D. in anthropology, Raymond Buckland, and his wife, who practice their craft in New York City, where Dr. Buckland edits manuals for an overseas airline; and Mrs. Florence S. (like the Air Force captain, she prefers anonymity), a Brooklyn housewife who owns a black cat named Thirteen.

Satanism is one of the most obscure manifestations of witchcraft. Several years ago Anton Szandor LaVey founded the First Satanic Church in San Francisco, dedicated to sensual indulgence, vengeance, and all sins. Mr. LaVey decries "good" witches; he preaches evil and wields black magic. (His "church" isn't open to visitors: telephone inquirers are told that they must first read the *Satanic Bible;* then, if they are in agreement with its teachings, they may make written application for membership.)

There are also mediums who specialize in communication with the dead. The late Bishop James A. Pike—in evident soul agony over his son Jim's suicide—consulted mediums in England and the United States, and was sufficiently convinced of the reality of an unseen spirit world to write a book about it, *The Other Side.*

Dr. Pike's book is just one of many publications in the field. A local bookstore has such recent titles as *Astrology for Everyday Living; Astrology Made Practical; Fortune-Telling With Cards; Dreams and Your Horoscope; Your Character in the Stars; Numerology; Your Future in Your Hand; Astrology Answers Your Questions; Astrology, Mythology, and the Bible; Astrology and Your Destiny; The Tarot Revealed;* and *Your Sun Personality.*

Then there are specialized books: *Your Baby's First Horoscope; Astrology for Teens;* and *How to Find Your Mate Through Astrology,* all of a personal nature. *Astrological Guide to Good Health; Five-Year Diet and Health Horoscope; Cooking With Astrology* and *Zodiac Cookbook* are for those who want health advice. For those whose concerns go beyond themselves, there are *Astrol-*

ogy and the United States, and *The Birdfeather Astrological Space Book.*

In a class all their own are *Astrology for Hounds* and *Cat Horoscope Book.*

The paperback horoscope business has exploded in the last few years. Each book in a series on signs of the Zodiac has sold 2.5 to 3 million copies every year, according to *The New York Times.* In its life of less than two years, Doubleday's occult Universe Book Club has attracted over 100,000 members from all ages, localities, sexes.

One hundred thousand gamblers bought *Astrology and Horse Racing* last year.

A Bantam sales executive says that the market for his company's occult line is primarily in the Bible Belt and the Deep South.

What's it all about? Why this flowering of the occult in an age of science, of the most universal— perhaps the best—system of mass education in history?

If someone knows what is in my future, whether it's today as I travel to work or the way my life will end, I'd like to find out about it, I think. If constellations can be good or bad for me, if my decisions may be enlightened by advice from those who know my time of birth, this is important. I think I'd like to know about it.

I say "I think" because I'm not really sure. There's a mystery to life's code, its unknown hours and days, that I'm not sure I'd want broken, even if an expert could do so. And there's a mystery in the beyond that could make me hold back from communicating with members of my family who have died, even if a medium could call them up.

But life at best is tough and death is inexorable. So I'd like to know whether these things are possible, whether help is available if I want it.

Are horoscopes and related phenomena one big put-on, or are they actual means of knowing the future, of taking steps beyond ourselves?

2. CAN STARS FORETELL THE FUTURE?

PART OF being a man is to wonder what will happen tomorrow. Will it be a good day to hunt or invest in a stock, to take a wife or go to war? Will the year ahead be happy, or will there be some disaster—perhaps a fire will sweep through the forest, or an earthquake will send the coastline crumbling into the ocean?

Primitive man "read" the intestines or liver of a slain animal, observed signs in the weather, followed a variety of folk superstitions to foretell the future and avoid trouble.

But then man began to look up from animals, fire and rain, to the stars. And he has continued to look up, even today, when people in cities seldom see the unobstructed heavens.

Blue sky, sun, dark sky, moon, stars and planets, clouds, lightning, thunder: these are the common mystical elements of a pastoral life. In primitive societies, man has found in them objects of worship.

Night has its special mystery. Despite our sophisticated knowledge of astronomy today we still have an emotional reaction to the night sky as we stand silent on Colorado mountain or Arizona desert.

Without the knowledge we possess, and without

lights to interrupt the darkness, primitive man was conscious of a deeper mystery in the night. This was the time when ghosts of dead men walked about, the time when witches were at work. And above all, night was the time when stars silently followed their tracks through darkened sky, when the moon moved and grew and waned in a pattern all its own.

In their beginnings, astronomy and astrology were one superstitious science, or scientific superstition. An astronomer-priest was probably responsible for the massive, mysterious Stonehenge boulders that have stood silent for 3500 years on Salisbury Plain in southern England. And such a priest, or astronomer, probably constructed the elaborate pre-Columbian Nazca sand drawings, with their calendar of the skies, that can be seen from an airplane, etched into the hillsides of southern Peru.

Astrology had its origin almost five thousand years ago in Mesopotamia. From Babylonia and Assyria, the exciting idea that stars foretell, predetermine the future traveled to Egypt, Greece and the East.

More primitive methods of predicting the future continued to be practiced even after astrology became ascendant. But astrology probably won the field because stars, moon, sun and planets could be depended on. Change and decay might be the rule of earthly life; the heavens were different. People who had no idea of the stars' distance or size could still appreciate their brightness, their perfect circles of orbit, and their orderly schedules.

13

Babylonians invented the zodiac, an imaginary orbit of fixed stars that occurs in the course of a year. The zodiac was divided into 12 "houses" which detailed the constellations of the stars. According to the astrological system, every house of the zodiac was ruled by a planet, and the sun was considered one of the planets.

The planets have been named for Greek and Roman gods, and are thought to possess individual characteristics similar to those of the gods. Sun, Moon, Jupiter and Venus are favorable to human endeavors; Saturn and Mars are unfavorable; while Mercury is somewhat ambivalent.

The signs of the zodiac (12 constellations) also have characteristics similar to their names. Capricorn (December 22–January 19) is the Goat; Aquarius (January 20–February 18) is the Water-bearer; Pisces (February 19–March 20) is the Fish; Aries (March 21–April 19) is the Ram; Taurus (April 20–May 20) is the Bull; Gemini (May 21–June 21) is The Twins; Cancer, delicately renamed by Carroll Righter, "Moonchildren," (June 22–July 22) is the Crab; Leo (July 23–August 22) is the Lion; Virgo (August 23–September 22) is the Virgin; Libra (September 23–October 23) is the Scales, for weighing; Scorpio (October 24–November 21) is the Scorpion; and Sagittarius (November 22–December 21) is the Archer.

Various stars are included in the astrologers' computations: Sirius, Antaras and Vega are among the more outstanding.

Relative positions of the planets within the house are important. Two planets in a direct radial line, or separated at most by a 10-degree angle, represent a "conjunction." Conjunctions of sun and moon are favorable, and so are various other angles, except for right angles and oppositions (180 degrees).

These represent the basic ingredients of astrology: 12 houses, seven planets, other stars and their relative positions. Additional elements—such as dividing the houses into 10 days—are introduced by the more sophisticated astrologers. Many different combinations of the ingredients are possible.

Position of the planets (and stars) in the celestial house on the date of birth is the critical factor that determines one's future. (Some, beginning with Pliny the Elder, have suggested that the day of conception would be more logical.)

Astrology is practiced worldwide today.

The late Hu Shih, Chinese philosopher, diplomat, and leader in the movement to make colloquial Chinese respectable, told of how his very existence was the result of an astrological omen.

Hu Shih's maternal grandparents were poor farmers who had a 17-year-old daughter. A neighbor, age 47, wanted their daughter's hand in marriage.

In a way, this was an unexpected request, since most girls at that time were engaged by the time they were 13 or 14. The prospective husband was an official who had traveled extensively, whose wife had died, leaving him with six children.

In the old Chinese calendar, the year, month, date and hour of birth are expressed by a total of eight written characters, and a horoscope is cast by taking these and, in the case of a proposed betrothal, comparing them with the eight characters of the other person.

Accordingly, through an intermediary, the official asked for the eight characters of the girl. These were given, but since the girl's mother was opposed to the match, she gave the wrong characters for date and time of birth.

The soothsayer realized that there had been a mistake or deception, so he looked up the correct characters. They matched perfectly with the prospective husband's, and the official and the farmer's daughter were married. Hu Shih was the result of their union.

Astrologers do not merely look to the stars and planets to predict the future; they believe that they cause what will happen in the future. The decisive influence on this earth, including human life, is exerted by the stars.

So the term "a born loser" may be an accurate description, according to this view. Or a born winner.

Not that the future is unchangeable. Bad prophecies may be averted by exercise of the individual's will; if the astrologer's claims are true, his great value is not merely to satisfy curiosity about the future, but to forewarn of impending trouble or even doom, so that diversionary tactics may be employed.

In theory, at least, horoscopes are prepared by believers in the system, using ancient knowledge about the positions of stars and planets in the zodiac.

But two problems at least are unresolved. Astrology has not accepted the Copernican theory;

it continues to be based on the faulty idea that stars and sun and planets move around the earth.

Astrologers still see the skies through the eyes of Middle Eastern viewers two thousand years ago.

Since 150 B.C., when the astrological system became crystalized, the zodiac has shifted by an entire house because of a gradual shift in the sun's apparent orbit through the stars. This throws each house's calculations off by one month, a serious defect that would seem to affect the reliability of every horoscope, if you go by the theoretical system.

Another is that people with the same birthday—born at the same time and in generally adjacent geographic areas—should have the same experiences in life if the stars determine those experiences. But except for male Virgos, born on September 14, first date to be drawn in the 1969 draft lottery, this is obviously not so.

But you can't argue with success. And the general view is that astrologers have been successful in foretelling events yet future, some of them highly significant. President John F. Kennedy's assassination, for instance, was predicted by Jeane Dixon. Richard M. Nixon's Presidency, a year and a half before the election and Jacqueline Kennedy's marriage to a non-American on foreign soil: both were foretold by British astrologer Maurice Woodruff.

And there are people at the office who will tell you they never should have left on a trip that day when their car was totaled: "Carroll Righter said events would move rapidly and the best course was to abstain from action."

Many horoscopes, especially those syndicated in newspapers, are similar to the Delphic Oracle of ancient Greece. For a fee, questions were answered by a "Pythia" or medium. Answers were subject to various interpretations, and seem to have been purposely obscure. Even today, a "Delphic pronouncement" is a statement that can be taken more than one way.

What about astrologers' goofs, their predictions that fail to materialize?

The California earthquake of April, 1969, was a monumental one. Astrologers warned that a large slice of California—some of them said the whole state—would fall into the Pacific Ocean as a result of a devastating earthquake. People moved away because of their faith in the prediction, and Governor Ronald Reagan had to issue a statement that he'd been planning for some time to take his vacation outside the State during April. What happened during April? Nothing.

On October 20, 1968, Jeane Dixon's syndicated column had to be hastily withdrawn from newspapers in which it would have appeared. Reason: Mrs. Dixon had written, "I still stand on my New Year's prediction and see no marriage for Jackie in the near future." That turned out to be the day of Jacqueline Kennedy's wedding to Aristotle Onassis.

British astrologer Maurice Woodruff claims 75 percent accuracy for his predictions. Like Jeane Dixon and Carroll Righter, he makes a lot of money. But it's by being paid to foretell the future of others, not by making investments in the light of the future for himself. Among his failures are the birth of a male child to Frank and Mia Sinatra —a year before they were divorced without any children; an overnight end to the Vietnam war in April, 1969 (Mrs. Dixon had already predicted peace in 1965); and the marriage of Lynda Bird Johnson to actor George Hamilton.

Astrology has become big business in the United States—how big nobody knows, although an estimated ten thousand Americans make their living by foretelling the future. This turn of events has occurred in the past 25 years; during World War II it was considered an oddity and an indication of his pagan beliefs that Adolf Hitler had an astrologer whom he consulted about personal matters and his conduct of the Third Reich.

In such a competitive business, perhaps we should expect spectacular failures as people try to outdo each other in getting public attention.

These failures do not automatically disprove the possibility of seeing into the world beyond, as various psychics and mediums are quick to remind us. But they must be considered in evaluating the reliability of predictions.

December 1, 1969, was a date of great significance to millions of young American men and their families: the first draft lottery was held that night.

In view of the astrologers' claims to know the future, it is interesting to note their predictions that day for men drawn first (to be called up almost immediately or immediately after their deferments end), and for those drawn last (who

19

will probably never be called, but be completely exempt from the draft). Remember that for the first group, the news was the worst possible; for the latter, the very best.

Here are excerpts from three astrology columns that day.

First drawn in the lottery (bad news), Virgos, born September 14: Jeane Dixon, *Chicago Tribune*: "You are close to your best today in material affairs if you will listen to the urging of your intuitive powers." Carroll Righter, *Chicago Daily News*: "Make plans for self-improvement in the near future." Ceean, *Chicago Sun Times*: "You may be faced with unexpected competition, but you can handle it just fine."

Last drawn (hooray!), Geminis, born June 7: Jeane Dixon: "Tonight hold a simple gathering of friends with different viewpoints." Carroll Righter: "Take it easy in the evening." Ceean: "Those around you are in an exuberant mood but it doesn't rub off on you."

The basic idea on which astrology is based— that the stars have a decisive influence on human affairs—has been rejected by serious scientists.

In 1949, the German Astronomical Society, one of the most respected in the world, dismissed astrology as a mixture of superstition, quackery and big business, adding that even those astrological circles which have rejected the stupidities of fairground astrology, and which consider themselves purely scientific associations, have never provided evidence of their scientific methods and results.

An American commission, under the chairmanship of the astronomer Bart J. Box of Harvard University, after having declared its readiness to test all cases submitted to them by astrologers, concluded that not a single one of the influences attributed to the stars by so-called serious astrologers could be demonstrated. Similar conclusions were reached by a Belgian committee, set up in 1949 by the Rector of Ghent University *(Comité Belge pour l'investigation scientifique des phénomènes reputés paranormaux)*, which consisted of 30 reputable scientists belonging to various fields.

Finally, according to the evidence of the American Society for Psychological Research (1940), "There is no evidence that astrology has any value whatever in revealing the past, the present or the future fate of any human being, and there is not the slightest reason for believing that social events can be predicted by astrology. Similar pronouncements have also been published by UNESCO and by many teachers, writers and scientists." (Richard Lewinsohn, *Prophets and Prediction)*.

That sort of unanimous scientific opinion should settle the matter once and for all for most thinking people, perhaps, but it doesn't. Who ever said that astrology was scientific in the first place? It's metaphysical, parapsychological, religious even. Or so astrologers answer. So it cannot be proved or disproved by telescopes and mathematics.

3. SATANISM

SAN FRANCISCO, Detroit and Toledo hardly seem like places where Satan would be at home. He belongs to the Garden of Eden, spoiling life for Adam and Eve; to the Judean Wilderness, tempting Jesus; to Berlin during the thirties and early forties, possessing Adolf Hitler.

But there he is, worshiped in these modern American cities.

Anton Szandor LaVey is high priest of San Francisco's "Church of Satan," where regular services are held. Black masses (perversions of the historic Roman Catholic mass) are celebrated, lectures on black magic are given to assembled witches, and divination and sorcery are practiced in a black-painted Victorian house on California Street.

Inside the house, a visitor is shown to a dimly lighted living room. Its walls are painted black, the ceiling red. A black coffin stands on end beside the fireplace; from its top a stuffed owl surveys the room. The fireplace mantle is the "living altar": a nude priestess reclines there during "church" services.

LaVey is a bad witch, preaching evil and practicing black magic. He has no time for good ones. "The one and only deadly sin in Satanism is self-deceit," he says. "Those who pussyfoot around are setting themselves up for bad news—using the devil's tools but not giving the devil his due."

According to LaVey, the late film star Jayne Mansfield asked him to hex her bothersome lover, Steve Brody. Shortly afterward, both Brody and Miss Mansfield died in an automobile accident, and LaVey allegedly claimed that the actress was an innocent victim of his curse.

Another incident involving LaVey and his "church" of Satan was reported in the press, when a young sailor—previously active in a Baptist church in Chicago, who later came under LaVey's influence— was buried with a Satanic funeral.

Herbert Arthur Sloane, high priest of the Toledo, Ohio, Satanic church, claims that he is not worshiping the biblical Satan. Instead, he brings the news that an "ultimate god" exists, "above and beyond the one that created the cosmos."

From the Judeo-Christian viewpoint, any god or gods who seek to usurp the one true God and worship of Him alone are *prima facie* Satanic, whether they admit it or not. "I am the Lord your God," Moses was told on Mount Sinai. "You shall have no other gods before me."

Satan's influence is therefore not to be evaluated only, or even primarily, on those rare occasions—such as the "churches" established by LaVey and Sloane—when he is deified and worshiped as God.

In the Bible and in history, he is more often hidden from view, inspiring others to imitate and carry out his plans. He is a "lion, seeking those whom he may devour," but he is also "an angel of

23

light," deceiving even those who belong to the true God.

Jeane Dixon is an example of the confusion Satan introduces to the present situation. A devout Roman Catholic, Mrs. Dixon's personal life is impeccable. She attributes her "gift" of prescience to a God-given psychic sensivity. Much of what she predicts seems to be theocentric, even Christocentric. Without doubt she scores high on extrasensory perception.

Yet there is a strangeness to some of her visions, a warning signal raised. For instance, she describes a dramatic vision on July 14, 1952, when a snake crawled onto her bed and coiled itself about her body.

"While I watched, it slowly turned its eyes and gazed into mine," she later reported. "In them was the all-knowing wisdom of the ages. . . . It did not speak, but I seemed to know that it was telling me that I had much to learn."

This account is too similar to the temptation of Eve in the Garden by Satan in the form of a serpent to leave us comfortable.

Satan is called "the god of this world [who] has blinded the minds of the unbelievers to keep them from seeing the light of the gospel of the glory of Christ, who is the likeness of God." (II Corinthians 4:4, *R.S.V.*)

A power for evil exists in this universe, according to the Bible (and confirmed by human experience). At various times in history that power has acted to thwart righteousness and justice. The time of Israel's enslavement in Egypt was one of those times; the time of Hitler's extermination of Jews was another.

Pharaoh and Hitler consulted their spiritists. So do many people today.

4. THIRTEEN WITCHES MAKE A COVEN

THE MYTH content of witchcraft is endlessly complicated. To bring order out of all its varieties, ancient and modern, seems almost impossible.

What are its common elements?

First is the person who wants something. He may be a migrant worker or the head of a nation. But he wants something that is beyond his grasp.

Second is what he wants, the object of his desire. This may be victory over his country's enemies, knowledge of what will happen in ten years —or tomorrow, sexual conquest, a winning number, healing, the sickness or death of a personal enemy. (It is wrong to assume that every desire of one who seeks a witch's mediation is evil. Some desires may be good, some bad.)

Third (the constitutive element of witchcraft) is the intermediary through whom he seeks to attain the object he wants. This mediator is a witch, who stands in the same relationship to the one who seeks him out as a priest stands in religion—which also is endlessly complicated in its varieties.

The mediator may be called a witch, or he may not. He may be called an astrologer, a Satanist, a fortune-teller, magician, conjurer, sorcerer, demonologist, palmist, card reader. Regardless of his title or the method he uses, he is an intermediary who exists to enable the seeker to find what he wants. (The term "medium" comes closest to describing the witch's essential mediating function.)

An intermediary between the seeker and what? What is the source of the power a witch claims to foretell the future, to establish contact with the dead?

The one person this is not is God. Witches do not claim to mediate between a seeking person and the divine being; if they did they would be priests rather than witches.

Whether they are as explicit as Anton LaVey—who asserts that his mediation is with Satan—or not, witches are in contact with the unseen powers of darkness rather than the powers of light, if they have any contact at all.

Witchcraft has probably been helped with the historic problem of its image by the recent movie *Rosemary's Baby*, and by the television series, *Bewitched*. The latter features a beautiful witch, Samantha.

There are good witches. But even they acknowledge the frailty of human flesh.

"People are searching," said Sybil Leek, in a *New York Times* interview. "They are searching for a religion where they don't have to live a Godlike life, a religion that acknowledges them as human beings."

To be a witch involves commitment, according to Mrs. Leek (as reported by the *Chicago Daily News*). "I did not just wake up one morning and discover I was a witch," she explains. "Witchcraft, like any other religion, must be accepted consciously. It is a decision that requires maturity." (The historic view of a witch was that he sold his soul to the devil in exchange for arcane powers.)

Secrecy surrounds the Craft, which is the way witches refer to their dark religion. *The Book of Shadows* is the Craft's bible; it contains spells, charms, rituals, chants and curses.

A coven is the standard unit of witchcraft. It consists of 12 witches (six male, six female) and a high priest or priestess. Meetings are held each month, usually when the moon is full, with eight festivals during the year. These festivals are called sabbaths, or sabbats. Major sabbats are held on Candlemas (February 2), May Eve (April 30), Lammas (July 31) and Hallowe'en, the really big one (October 31). Lesser ones are celebrated on spring and fall equinoxes, and summer and winter solstices.

Hallowe'en sabbat at the Bucklands' home on Long Island, New York, follows this pattern: "First the witches remove their clothes and bathe in salt water to purify themselves. Then, still nude (or 'skyclad,' as they call it), they descend to the basement and step inside a nine-foot circle that is drawn about them with a 400-year-old sword by Mrs. Buckland, the high priestess, who is known in the craft as Lady Rowen. A bewitching ambience is provided by music from a tape recorder and incense burned in a brass censer.

"Once inside the circle, the witches sing, chant, dance with broomsticks in commemoration of an ancient fertility rite, drink tea and wine, and listen to the high priestess read from the Book of Shadows.

"The ceremony ends after Lady Rowen, dressed only in a silver crown, bracelet, necklace and green leather garter belt, takes a horned helmet and places it on the head of her husband, the high priest, who is known as Robat. This signifies that power has been transferred from the high priestess who reigns during the six months of summer, to the high priest, who rules during the six winter months." *(The New York Times)*

Of course there are put-ons, people who are merely making a good thing out of America's current affair with the occult. They're in it for the money, they produce what consumers want, and they depend on laws of probability for the measure of success they enjoy. Their utterances are often Delphic.

Jeane Dixon may be this sort of person, although her writings seem sincere and she claims that God is the source of her prescience.

But if He is, His batting average on foretelling the future is low.

This is a major test of whether a person who predicts the future speaks from God or not, according to the Old Testament. Moses said, "When a prophet speaks in the name of the Lord, if the word does not come to pass or come true, that is a word which the Lord has not spoken; the prophet has spoken it presumptuously, you need not be afraid of him." (Deuteronomy 18, *R.S.V.)*

Another test of whether a prophet speaks for God or not is given by Moses in Deuteronomy 13 *(R.S.V.)*: "If a prophet arises among you, or a dreamer of dreams, and gives you a sign or a wonder, and the sign or wonder which he tells you comes to pass, and if he says, 'Let us go after other gods,' which you have not known, 'and let us serve them,' you shall not listen to the words of that prophet or to that dreamer of dreams; for the Lord your God is testing you, to know whether you love the Lord your God with all your heart and with all your soul."

When a man or woman claims to speak for God, to foretell the future on the basis of divine revelation, there is no margin for error. And what he says is to be tested by whether he turns his followers to the true God or not.

If he doesn't, God disowns him and his words.

Modern horoscopes (and other "revelations" from "the other side") do not measure up to what we would expect, if their source is God, in their thought content. If God speaks through Jeane Dixon, His daily revelations are quite pedestrian when contrasted to His revelations through Old Testament prophets. "Stand on your own feet and do what you find is well within your reach," says Mrs. Dixon.

God says (through Jeremiah): "If you have raced with men on foot, and they have wearied you, how will you compete with horses? And if in a safe land you fall down, how will you do in the jungle of the Jordan?"

5. WHEN HELL BROKE LOOSE IN SALEM

DURING THE WINTER of 1691–92, a small group of girls met at the home of Samuel Parris, minister of the church at Salem Village, Massachusetts. Elizabeth Parris was nine years old; the others— about nine of them—ranged in age from 11 to 20. All came from respected families.

Mr. Parris owned several slaves, probably brought by him from the West Indies, where he had been in business before coming to Massachusetts and taking the church. Two of them were husband and wife (John Indian and Tituba) who brought some knowledge of the black arts or superstitions, with them. They fascinated the teenage girls during winter afternoons with palmistry and fortune telling, necromancy, magic and spiritism.

Parris was hardly a model pastor. He was coarse and arrogant, and imposed severe church discipline for trivial offenses. By 1691 the factions into which the village was divided were ready to fly at each other's throats.

Under the training of John Indian and Tituba, the girls soon learned how to go into trances, talk gibberish and act in other strange ways.

A woman about thirty years old, mother of one of the girls, high-strung and deeply involved in church dissension and village quarrels, was the other main participant in what happened. She was Mistress Ann Putnam, wife of a respected village official.

During the days after Christmas, 1691, these girls discovered that they could interest and worry their adult elders with such tricks as crawling on the floor, going into fits or trances, and speaking unintelligible jargon. They came to be known as "the Afflicted Children."

Perhaps the serious interest in what they were doing led them to take the next step, which was to claim that they had been bewitched and couldn't help acting this way. Or they may have been afraid of parental punishment. Or John Indian and Tituba may have put them up to it. (If it was the latter, the suggestion soon boomeranged.)

When the girls claimed that witches had brought them under their power, Samuel Parris did two things: he sent his own daughter away from the village to live with friends; and he publicly commanded the others to name the witches.

The girls began by naming two forlorn old women and Tituba as their tormentors. Sarah Good was an especially apt choice, since there was a general willingness to receive any charge against her. Her neighbors considered her worthless, her husband had deserted her, and she was at times forced to wander from door to door with her children, seeking help. She had no house.

Here is the record of Sarah Good's examination, after she had been imprisoned in the Boston jail.

THE EXAMINATION OF SARAH GOOD BEFORE THE WORSHIPFUL ESQRS. JOHN HATHORNE AND JONATHAN CORWIN.

Q.   Sarah Good, what evil spirit have you familiarity with?

A.   None.

Q.   Why do you hurt these children?

A.   I do not hurt them. I scorn it.

Q.   Who do you employ then to do it?

A.   I employ nobody.

Q.   What creature do you employ then?

A.   No creature: but I am falsely accused.

Q.   Why did you go away muttering from Mr. Parris's house?

A.   I did not mutter, but I thanked him for what he gave my child.

Q.   Have you made no contract with the devil?

A.   No.

Hathorne next desired the ["afflicted"] children, all of them, the woman's accusers, to look upon her, and see if this were the person that hurt them; and so they did all look upon her, and said this was one of the persons that did torment them. Presently they were all tormented [screams, writhing, gibberish, etc.]

Q.   Sarah Good, do you not see now what you have done? Why do you not tell us the truth? Why do you thus torment these poor children?

A.   I do not torment them.

Q.   Who do you employ then?

A.   I employ nobody. I scorn it.

Q.   How came they thus to be tormented?

A.   What do I know? You bring others here, and now you charge me with it.

Q.   Why, who was it?

A.   I do not know, but it was some you brought into the meeting-house with you.

Q.   We brought you into the meeting house.

A.   But you brought in two more.

Q.   Who was it then, that tormented the children?

A.   It was Osburn [the other white woman].

Q.   What is it you say when you go muttering away from persons' houses?

A.   If I must tell, I will tell.

Q.   Do tell us then.

A.   If I must tell, I will tell: it is the Commandments. I may say my Commandments, I hope.

Q.   What Commandment is it?

A.   If I must tell you, I will tell: it is a psalm.

Q.   What psalm?

A.   (After a long time she muttered over some part of a psalm.)

Q.   Who do you serve?

A.   I serve God.

Q.   What God do you serve?

A.   The God that made heaven and earth.

Her answers were in a very wicked, spiteful manner, reflecting and retorting against the authority with base and abusive words; and many lies she was taken in. It was here said that her husband had said that he was afraid that she either was a witch or would be one very quickly. The worshipful Mr. Hathorne asked him his reason why he said so of her, whether he had ever

34

seen anything by her. He answered, "No, not in this nature," but it was her bad carriage to him; "and indeed," said he, "I may say with tears, that she is an enemy to all good."

The foregoing was in the handwriting of Ezekiel Cheever. Following are comments by John Hathorne, one of the two magistrates.

Salem Village, March the first, 1692

Sarah Good, upon examination, denied the matter of fact (*viz.*) that she ever used any witchcraft, or hurt the abovesaid children, or any of them.

The abovenamed children, being all present, positively accused her of hurting them sundry times within this two months, and also that morning. Sarah Good denied that she had been at their houses in said time or near them, or had done any hurt. All the abovesaid children then present then accused her face to face; upon which they were all dreadfully tortured and tormented for a short space of time [in the meeting-house courtroom] and, the affliction and torture being over, they charged said Sarah Good again that she had then so tortured them, and came to them and did it, although she was personally then kept [in the courtroom] at considerable distance from them.

Sarah Osburn maintained her innocence during subsequent questioning; but Tituba declared herself guilty and accused the other two of having been in league with the Devil with her. When she confessed, the teen-age girls subsided and were quiet for the first time.

The women were remanded to Boston jail, where they were kept in chains. Mrs. Osburn died less than three months later.

The teen-age girls had now experienced notoriety and power. They could hardly be expected to return from this pinnacle to ordinary housework and afternoon group meetings.

So a series of accusations and trials began. From the lowliest women in the village they moved to the most respected, the most saintly. And they even accused Sarah Good's daughter, Dorcas, "between four and five years old."

When the little girl was led into the courtroom for questioning, three of the girls charged her with biting, pinching and almost choking them. They showed marks that they claimed were of her teeth on their arms; they shrieked with pain, and pins with which they said she pierced them were discovered on their bodies.

The evidence was considered conclusive. Dorcas, not yet five years old, was remanded to Boston jail with her mother, where she was probably chained, too. Extraordinary fastenings were thought necessary to hold a witch.

When saintly women, in old age, and even a clergyman were accused, Salem village fell apart. Suspicion and malice reigned; no one trusted his neighbor.

Before the matter ended, nineteen persons were hanged, in addition to Mrs. Osburn, who died of ill-treatment in prison. Many more—as many as

160—were imprisoned, some ruined by their experience.

After it had all blown over, Tituba said that her master, Reverend Samuel Parris, beat her and otherwise abused her, to make her confess and accuse (as he claimed) her sister-witches. When it came time for her release, Parris refused to pay the jailer for her room and board, and she was sold to a new slave-owner for these costs.

One of the wretched children, Ann Putnam, humbled herself 14 years later before the church in Salem, when she was 26 years old. She declared that, with others, she had been instrumental in bringing upon the land the guilt of innocent blood, "though what was said or done by me against any person, I can truly and uprightly say before God and man, I did it not out of any anger, malice, or ill-will to any person, for I had no such thing against any one of them, but what I did was ignorantly, being deluded of Satan."

The Salem witch trials are a classic example of mass hysteria, the sort of social movement that occasionally appears in history and blots the page. Hitler's persecution and destruction of Jews had many similar elements.

The incident is also one that confirms C. S. Lewis's statement, "Those who are readiest to die for a cause may easily become those who are readiest to kill for it." *(Reflections on the Psalms,* Harcourt-Brace)

But underneath the event runs a stream of darkness, in Ann Putnam's words, "a delusion of Satan."

Who were the Salem witches? We might suggest that they were John Indian and Tituba, and the teen-age girls who learned from them their spirit craft, rather than the Christian women who were accused, imprisoned, and—in some instances— hanged.

Salem was too much for the New World to stomach. Salem drove witchcraft underground for almost three centuries of "Enlightenment."

Now it's been exhumed on a new winter's afternoon before the fire, as fun and games.

This game could hurt us all before it ends.

FRENCH PSYCHOLOGIST P. Janet describes a man possessed by a demon: "He murmured blasphemies in a deep and solemn voice: 'Cursed be God,' he said, 'cursed the Trinity, cursed the Virgin.' . . . Then in a higher voice and with eyes full of tears: 'It is not my fault if my mouth says these horrible things, it is not I. . . . It is not I. . . . I press my lips together so that the words may not come through, may not break forth, but it is useless; the devil then says these words inside me, I feel plainly that he says them and forces my tongue to speak in spite of me.' The demon twisted his arms and legs and made him endure cruel sufferings which wrung horrible cries from the wretched man." (*Nevroses et idées fixes*)

This description reminds us of some New Testament examples of possession. Among them is one recorded in Mark 9 (*R.S.V.*):

And one of the crowd answered him, "Teacher, I brought my son to you, for he has a dumb spirit; and wherever it seizes him, it dashes him down; and he foams and grinds his teeth and becomes rigid; and I asked your disciples to cast it out, and they were not able.

And he answered them, "O faithless generation, how long am I to be with you? How long am I to bear with you? Bring him to me."

And they brought the boy to him; and when the spirit saw him, immediately it convulsed the boy, and he fell on the ground and rolled about, foaming at the mouth.

And Jesus asked his father, "How long has he had this?"

And he said, "From childhood. And it has often cast him into the fire and into the water, to destroy him; but if you can do anything, have pity on us and help us."

And Jesus said to him, "If you can! All things are possible to him who believes."

Immediately the father of the child cried out and said, "I believe; help my unbelief!"

And when Jesus saw that a crowd came running together, he rebuked the unclean spirit, saying to it, "You dumb and deaf spirit, I command you, come out of him, and never enter him again."

And after crying out and convulsing him terribly, it came out, and the boy was like a corpse; so that most of them said, "He is dead." But Jesus took him by the hand and lifted him up, and he arose.

And when he had entered the house, his disciples asked him privately, "Why could we not cast it out?"

And he said to them, "This kind cannot be driven out by anything but prayer."

A German observer presents a patient's own description of such an experience (J. Kerner, *Nachricht von dem ältester Kirchengeschichte*):

40

The Evil One who was hidden within me began to rage again. I was obliged almost without ceasing to utter cries, weep, sing, dance, and roll upon the ground where I went into horrible contortions. I was forced to jerk my head and feet in all directions, howl like a bear and also utter the cries of other animals, things which had, moreover, all happened before on previous occasions.

I strove vigorously (on the doctor's instigation) to repress the fits, but only succeeded at the end of fourteen days and solely by the help and prayers of a dear and very pious woman.

I am never absent, I always know what I am doing and saying, but I cannot always express what I wish; there is something within me which prevents it. In the most furious fits I dare not offer the slightest resistance, for I should only make myself more unhappy, and force is, moreover, of no avail; it is therefore voluntarily that I give myself up to the power of the Evil One, and let him rage, for it is only so that I can once more get a little rest.

The reality of demon possession is taught in both Old and New Testaments. Demons are invisible, but real, spiritual beings who are under the control of Satan, "prince of the devils."

This was a special sickness, not a term loosely used for any disease that produced seizures. Demonism is distinguished from other diseases in Matthew 4:24, "They brought [Jesus] all the sick, those afflicted with various diseases and pains, demoniacs, epileptics, and paralytics, and he healed them."

41

Centuries of enlightenment in the Judeo-Christian religion may explain why demon possession is seldom diagnosed in the United States and Canada today, even by Christian psychiatrists, although it is recognized in pagan cultures.

The greatest care must be exercised not to describe mental conditions as demonic in origin. But this does not mean that even today some may not be "bound by Satan" through possession by demons.

Some years ago, I had a pastoral relationship with a man who was then, and had been for several years, under a psychiatrist's care. He had been institutionalized on two different occasions, was in deep depression, and had tried to commit suicide three times by bizarre means. Each time he was discovered and saved, rather remarkably.

His illness culminated in an act of violence in which property was destroyed, although no one was injured.

Papers were prepared for his commitment to a state hospital.

When I talked with him, he said, "You know that group therapy and shock treatments aren't going to help me."

I said that I knew no such thing; I wasn't a physician or psychiatrist.

"Well, they won't. You know what's the matter with me."

"How can I know?" I replied.

"You do."

"What is wrong with you, do you think?"

"You know."

"No, I don't."

42

"Yes, you do."

I had begun to suspect that he meant demon possession, so I asked, "Do you want me to pray for you?"

"Yes, please do. It's my only hope."

I prayed that God, who knows all things, would rebuke the demon, if indeed my friend was possessed. I told God that I didn't know whether he was or not, but I was praying this at his request. And I asked God to deliver my friend by the blood of His Son, shed on the cross to redeem sinners and defeat Satan.

He was not committed to the state hospital. In a short time he took up the responsibilities and cares of job and home again, and weathered some great crises (not related to his mental illness) without depression or suicide attempts.

That was years ago. Today he is normal in every way.

I merely report an incident that may or may not have been demonic in origin, but from which I believe God delivered my friend.

G. Campbell Morgan, minister of Westminster Chapel in London, believed that demonic activity is responsible for the upsurge during this century of spiritualistic phenomena (witches, sorcerers, mediums, etc.). Dr. Morgan felt that where one of these terms is employed, "demonized" man or woman may properly be substituted.

Possession follows a variety of patterns.

The possession of persons Jesus healed was involuntary. They were in bondage not of their own choice.

Voluntary possession (sometimes referred to as

"selling one's soul to the devil") may not be susceptible to help.

Robert Lewis Stevenson's *The Strange Case of Dr. Jekyll and Mr. Hyde* chronicles a classic case of possession in literature. Mr. Hyde became a person with a new self-consciousness, different from that of Dr. Jekyll. In this type of possession, the appearance is changed, the voice often changes, personality undergoes radical change for the worse. Harmful acts may be committed, either against the possessed person himself, or against others, blasphemies and obscenities may be spoken.

A different kind of possession is found in the person who is a spectator, watching his own actions during a seizure. He may speak of himself in the third person.

Voodoo is a fairly recent branch of occult religion, although its roots are in African religions. It is found mainly in Haiti.

It thrives among the poor and disadvantaged. Voodoo doesn't promise riches or pleasure, but rather aims at removing the nagging miseries of life: for instance, sickness and misfortune, which are considered divine judgments.

A priest or priestess demands absolute submission to his authority for adherents to voodoo. Worship is carried on in a sanctuary.

One significant characteristic of voodoo belief is that spirits can incarnate themselves in people they choose. Any voodoo worshiper can therefore enter into contact with the unseen world. The person becomes a mere receptacle for the spirit, a shell of flesh to contain it. Voodoo priests believe they can bring this about.

Thus people can be changed into animals, even.

Trancelike states are often a part of voodoo worship. Spells are cast on an enemy; a special spell is "sending of the dead," by which a dead person is sent to prey on an enemy. This may cause sickness and death.

Our light and frivolous approach to the unseen spirit world today, our craze for horoscopes and mediums, fortune-tellers and Ouija boards—turning it all into one big game—may be an open invitation to Satan and his demons to come out into the open in our society, to fill the vacuum of spirit that exists.

To turn from light is to turn to darkness. To turn from God is to turn to Satan. To turn from love is to turn to fear.

Friedrich Nietzsche described the *cultus* in which demonism grows, in this section from *Joyful Wisdom:*

Have you not heard of that madman who, on a bright morning, lit a lantern and went out into the market place and cried unceasingly: "I seek God!"

And at that minute there were many present who did not believe in God and, therefore, they made mocking laughter.

"Has He gone astray?" said one of the crowd.

"Has He run too far, like a child, and got lost?" asked another.

"Or perhaps He is hiding."

"Or is He frightened of us?"

"Maybe He has gone on an ocean voyage."

"Or did He emigrate to another country?"

Thus they shouted and laughed confusedly to one another.

The madman threw himself among them and his gaze penetrated them through and through. "Where has God gone to?" he asked loudly. "I will tell you. We killed Him, you and I. We are all of us His murderers.

"But how did we do this? How could we drink the sea to its dregs? Who has given us the sponge to erase the whole horizon? What have we done by cutting ourselves off from that which bindeth earth to its sun? Where shall it now revolve? Where shall we move? Away from all suns? Do we not fall headlong without ceasing? Backwards and sidewards, forwards, in all directions. Is there still an above and a below? Do we not stray as though in endless void? Does not the empty space blow into our faces? Has it not become colder now? Does not night come on ever more and ever more night? Do we not have to light lanterns in the forenoon?

"God is dead. God will remain dead. And we killed Him! How shall we console ourselves, the most murderous of all murderers?"

7. EXTRA-SENSORY PERCEPTION

MOST OF US have seen a mind-reader perform his magic on stage. We know there is some explanation for what he is able to do, even as there's an explanation for such tricks as pulling a rabbit out of a hat or sawing a woman in half.

But is there reality behind the tricks of mental telepathy? Do some people possess unusual power to see the unseen, to penetrate the mind of others, to predict the future?

For many years, experimentation has been going on in the fields of mental telepathy and extra-sensory perception.

An experiment in thought-transference involving two sisters was reported as early as 1883 by W. F. Gurney *et al.* When investigated by a committee, the Creery sisters performed various feats, including identification of playing cards turned up at random by the research team.

The advantage of such experiments with playing cards is that the likelihood of successful guesses is known, in the absence of factors that would favor correct guesses (connivance between the principals, poor shuffling from previous order, etc.). In a random drawing, the chance is one in 52 of guessing the correct card.

Subsequent to the report on the Creery sisters'

high scores in guessing, it was found that they sometimes used a system of signals. In spite of their protestations that they only resorted to this if they didn't want to disappoint visitors during a run of wrong guesses, and that experiments with the best results were not influenced by signals, this revelation took the edge off these early experiments.

When Professor J. B. Rhine began his experiments at Duke University in 1927, he chose to use a pack of 25 cards, five each of five different kinds: star, cross, circle, square, waves. Possibility of successful guessing was improved from one in 52 (deck of playing cards) to one in five. This did not affect the validity of results, however.

At the beginning of Rhine's experiments, he had one person look at the card while another guessed, as in the Creery experiments. Mental telepathy (ability to transfer thoughts without the usual sensory channels of communication) seemingly explained unusual success. Later, when he tested successful guessers without prior examination of the cards by an observer, Dr. Rhine found that correct guesses were still above normal.

This led to the extra-sensory perception (E.S.P.) theory: some people have the ability to know, by beyond-normal means, facts of the external world hidden to them, without the necessity of these facts being transmitted from someone's mind. Mental telepathy depends on another person's having the fact in his mind; E.S.P. does not.

A further step was taken in the Rhine experiments. Successful guessers, who had high scores on identifying cards before they were turned over and seen by anybody, were told to predict on paper the future order of a pack of E.S.P. cards before they were even shuffled. Then, after the pack was shuffled and cut in a random fashion, the actual order of the cards was compared to the predicted order. Some subjects had an above-normal degree of success in foretelling an order that did not yet exist, which is referred to as precognition.

Children seem to score better in such extra-sensory perception experiments than adults, the uneducated better than highly educated people. A. A. Foster reports that primitive Canadian Indian children were far ahead of highly intelligent London college students.

While research in the E.S.P. field seems to establish the possibility of perceiving facts not available to the senses, the level of such perception is hardly to be compared to highly sophisticated incidents reported by some researchers.

Joost A. M. Meerloo, associate professor of psychiatry at New York School of Psychiatry, gives the following case study:

A patient in psychotherapy brings to the therapeutic session a frightening dream in which he saw that his younger brother had a car accident. He never dreams about his brother nor about car accidents. The therapist writes the dream down and tries to find out why this patient had that tragic inner vision that night. Though we do not yet understand the dream, the subject of our investigation is the strange ambivalent relation between the patient and his brother. A few days later the news comes in,

49

that the patient's brother who lives at 3,000 miles distance, was indeed the victim of a car accident at the very hour the dream was dreamt. Several visual traits in the dream correspond remarkably with the report of the accident.

Now begins the epistemological problem of how to judge this spontaneous case. Is it merely a coincidence? Every theoretician of probability would laugh at such a supposition. Are we satisfied in saying in full awe: "This was again that mysterious psi-factor?" Or can we, out of the therapeutic situation, learn to understand better why the brother in mortal danger sends out a message to our patient? Both brothers had had a very intensive emotional relation after the early death of their father, thereby repressing completely their early sibling rivalry. The depression for which my patient had come under treatment had been partly provoked by his younger brother's departure for California.

Something becomes now clinically more clear. The brothers had lived so close together as if they had been mutually dependent twins; especially among twins we are familiar with the fact that they can read each other's thoughts. Scientifically speaking, nothing is proved yet, but we have got an initial hunch about a broken rapport and communication that tries to reconstitute itself at a moment of extreme emergency.

Our group gathered many such examples of well-controlled dream material, its content corresponding with occurrences taking place far away. Parapsychological literature relates also plenty of these cases. Examples of mothers who experience the death of their sons on the battlefield in a specific dream are legion. During my own escape from the Nazis I noted down various informing dreams I had myself. (*Hidden Communion*)

What is our response to these examples?

Most of us just don't know how to respond. To agree that such communication takes place outside ordinary sensory experience is to admit the existence of a world and forces we cannot see.

Perhaps, just perhaps, there are senders and receivers, people who have strong E.S.P. The rest of us, if we deny the possibility, could be in the position of a person who has never seen television, who is told that images and sounds surround him, needing only to be channeled through a receiver to be seen and heard.

He won't believe it, for he's never experienced the reality.

In the whole field of parapsychology, a mystery exists that never seems to be fully removed by occasional evidence of deception and fraud.

Strange rappings in the night, objects moved without human or other visible intervention, the sense of a presence unseen but real: phenomena of this sort are documented to the point of strong evidence for their existence.

This is a different matter from the question whether stars rule human affairs and earth's destiny. Even without our Judeo-Christian presuppositions, we could not believe that lifeless masses of matter—including the moon on which men have walked—can be the source of information about the future.

A roach in a clock factory would hardly consider his destiny ruled by the mechanisms and machines above, around, beneath him—unless he was a very stupid or disturbed insect.

J. B. Phillips, British author and Bible translator, tells of an experience that cannot be explained by ordinary sensory data:

Many of us who believe in what is technically known as the Communion of Saints must have experienced the sense of nearness, for a fairly short time, of those whom we love soon after they have died. This has certainly happened to me several times. But the late C. S. Lewis, whom I did not know very well and had only seen in the flesh once, but with whom I had corresponded a fair amount, gave me an unusual experience. A few days after his death, while I was watching television, he "appeared" sitting in a chair within a few feet of me, and spoke a few words which were particularly relevant to the difficult circumstances through which I was passing. He was ruddier in complexion than ever, grinning all over his face and, as the old-fashioned saying has it, positively glowing with health. The interesting thing to me was that I had not been thinking about him at all. I was neither alarmed nor surprised nor, to satisfy the Bishop of Woolwich, did I look up to see the hole in the ceiling that he might have made on arrival! He was just *there*—"large as life and twice as natural." A week later, this time when

I was in bed, reading before going to sleep, he appeared again, even more rosily radiant than before, and repeated to me the same message, which was very important to me at the time. I was a little puzzled by this, and I mentioned it to a certain saintly bishop who was then living in retirement here in Dorset. His reply was, "My dear J————, this sort of thing is happening all the time." (*Ring of Truth*)

THE MOST FAMOUS astrologer in history was probably Nostradamus.

Michel Nostradamus, the celebrated French seer, physician and astrologer, was born in a small town south of Avignon, in 1503. He was the son of a notary public (a more significant office then than now). His grandfather taught him mathematics and astronomy.

Soon after he had completed his medical training, a great plague broke out. Nostradamus saved many people from dying; he could not save his own wife and children.

Suffering was a potent force in maturing the young physician's ideas.

In the attic of his house at Salon (after remarriage to a wife who bore his six children), Nostradamus had a special room where he observed the stars. Calculating orbits and conjunctions, he tried to foresee the future, writing down his predictions.

Nostradamus' celebrated work was published in 1555. Its success was so great that King Henry II invited the author to become part of his court. Nostradamus accepted, and spent the next eleven years moving in royal circles. He died at the age of 63, having—according to the record—predicted the hour of his death.

Here is how Nostradamus began his book of prophecies:

Absorbed in Nature's mysteries, I spend my nights,
In lonely solitude on seer's throne of brass
But soon the forlorn little flame makes me hope
That my faith will be rewarded.

When I hold the wand in my hands
The wave soon moistens my feet and the hem of
    my garments
I listen to a Voice and turn pale.
The heavenly light, the Divine inspiration, has
    come over me.

Nostradamus' work is divided into ten "Centuriates," each of which consists of one hundred quatrains (like those just given). The language is strange and obscure, but plain enough for followers of the prophet to claim that more than one hundred predictions have already been fulfilled.

Central in these prophecies is the history of France and Europe. Order is missing, either chronological or logical. Dates are given in only a few instances, but—according to Nostradamus —this was intentional.

Here are a few examples of his predictions, with the interpretations that were later given.

In the deepest part of Western Europe
A child will be born of poor parents
Who by his language will seduce the great army.
His fame will increase further because of a
        government expedition toward the East.

An Emperor will be born near Italy
Who will cost the Empire dearly.
Those with whom he allies himself will refer to
    him
As a butcher rather than a prince.

From the town near the sea from which contribu-
    tions are levied.
The shorn head will remove the satrapy,
Chasing away the dirt-mongers who oppose him.
For fourteen years he will retain the tyrant's
       scepter.

    These quatrains are understood to be predictions
of Napoleon's life and rule, more than two hundred
years before the incidents occurred.

    Napoleon was born in Corsica ("near Italy").
Contrary to prevailing fashion, he wore his hair
closely cut ("shorn head"). The British occupied
Toulon ("town near the sea"), and Napoleon ruled
a few months more than "fourteen years."

    The disastrous Russian expedition is supposedly
predicted by this quatrain:

A large fire will be seen in the direction of the
    rising sun,
Rumor and the bright light point to Aquilon.
Death and the cry of death rule all around
The aggressors will perish by the sword, through
    fire and starvation.

    More recent events are also claimed by adher-
ents to Nostradamus' predictions. The following

quatrain was pin-pointed as referring to World
War I. Notice the reference to submarines.

Gold and silver are fused by lightning in the arc,
The two prisoners will devour one another.
The greatest of the extensive city,
When the fleet, submerged, will swim.

Does the following quatrain predict the abortive
League of Nations experiment? Nostradamus buffs
claim it did.

The speeches delivered by the shores
    of Lake Geneva will cause annoyance.
Days will be shortened for weeks on end,
And even for months and years. Then all will
    secede.
The governments will condemn the meaningless
    statutes.

If we accept these examples (and many others)
as valid predictions that were later fulfilled, how
do we explain Nostradamus' strange power?

Nostradamus himself spoke of "voices" reaching
him from heaven, and the "divine splendor of the
exhibition of light." These references are without doubt to astrology, with its dependence on the
stars. But they may be a claim to more than that,
since the prophet was a devout Christian (in the
sense that these words were understood in the
16th century).

God was recognized by Nostradamus in the
preface to his prophecies as the source of all power;

therefore God must inspire a man before he can understand the future.

The astrologer also warned, in the words of "the true Savior," against casting pearls before swine. And he acknowledged that man cannot "know the times or seasons" which God has reserved to His own knowledge alone.

But Nostradamus departed from the Judeo-Christian Scriptures in believing that God chooses to rule man's destiny on earth through the influence of stars and constellations. The revelations he had about the future came in this way, Nostradamus believed, because God had thus ordained it.

But the Bible teaches something different about foretelling future events from the stars.

God warned His people, the Jewish nation, through Moses against turning for guidance about the present or future to any other source than Himself.

"Do not turn to mediums or wizards; do not seek them out, to be defiled by them: I am the Lord your God. . . . If a person turns to mediums and wizards, playing the harlot after them, I will set my face against that person, and will cut him off from among his people." (Leviticus 19, 20, R.S.V.)

"When you come into the land which the Lord your God gives you, you shall not learn to follow the abominable practice of those nations. There shall not be found among you any one who . . . practices divination, a soothsayer, or an augur, or a sorcerer, or a charmer, or a medium, or a wizard, or a necromancer. For whoever does these things is an abomination to the Lord; and because of these abominable practices the Lord your God is driving them out before you. You shall be blameless before the Lord your God. For these nations, which you are about to dispossess, give heed to soothsayers and to diviners; but as for you, the Lord your God has not allowed you so to do." (Deuteronomy 18, *R.S.V.*)

Later in Old Testament history, during the monarchy, God pronounced judgment against His people through His prophet Isaiah: "Evil shall come upon you, for which you cannot atone; disaster shall fall upon you, which you will not be able to expiate; and ruin shall come on you suddenly, of which you know nothing.

"Stand fast in your enchantments and your many sorceries, with which you have labored from your youth; perhaps you may be able to succeed, perhaps you may inspire terror. You are wearied with your many counsels; let them stand forth and save you, those who divide the heavens, who gaze at the stars, who at the new moons predict what shall befall you.

"Behold, they are like stubble, the fire consumes them; they cannot deliver themselves from the power of the flame. No coal for warming oneself is this, no fire to sit before! Such to you are those with whom you have labored, who have trafficked with you from your youth; they wander about each in his own direction; there is no one to save you." (Isaiah 47: 11-15, *R.S.V.*)

9. WHAT DID BISHOP PIKE REALLY HEAR?

I HAD A BRIEF acquaintance with James A. Pike in 1950, soon after he became chaplain of Columbia University in New York.

Prior to this, Dr. Pike was Episcopal chaplain at Vassar College. In this capacity, he had brought Reverend Bryan Green, Anglican priest and former chaplain of Oxford University, to Vassar for some evangelistic meetings.

The results were hardly what either man expected. They were attacked in religion classes and in the student newspaper for daring to imply that being a Christian involves objective belief rather than mere attitude. "Why, Mohandas Gandhi is as good a Christian as Reverend Bryan Green" was one comment that represented a general response.

Like most campus upsets (even in the late forties, when they were less usual than they are today), this one would probably have quieted down if Dr. Pike had not given it greater exposure. This he did in *The Living Church,* a national Episcopal laymen's magazine.

Without naming the college, although his restraint accomplished little since Pike was known to be Episcopal student worker at Vassar, Dr. Pike described what had happened. He went into some detail, explaining, for instance, that this former Oxford chaplain had been called a "Holy Roller" at the college. Dr. Pike concluded by expressing surprise that parents in the church who would never think of sending their daughters to a school that had an unbalanced diet in the dining hall, didn't think twice about sending them away to a school with a thoroughly unbalanced religious diet in the classroom.

Instantly, on publication, Dr. Pike became *persona non grata* to the Vassar authorities. He left his post there, only to be offered the much more significant position of university chaplain and head of the religion department at Columbia. (This was shortly after Dwight D. Eisenhower became president of the university.)

This was when I was introduced to him. (I was a Protestant student worker at the time, with responsibility for various colleges and universities in the East.)

We had conversations about Christian doctrine. Dr. Pike told me about his own conversion from humanistic agnosticism to faith in Jesus Christ, through the Episcopal Church, while he was serving as a government lawyer in Washington.

"I can't show favoritism in my position here," he told me, "but I'd rather see you get through to students than a theologically liberal movement, because you're getting them related to God."

We discussed such doctrines as man's fallen condition, the redemptive work of Jesus Christ, the work of the Holy Spirit. On these doctrines we were in close agreement with the biblical position.

Hearing the account of Dr. Pike's own conversion, and his doctrinal views, I had no doubt that we shared common faith and fellowship in Jesus Christ. Only recently since reading his book, *The Other Side*, have questions been raised in my mind by such a statement as this: "It is not unlike saying the Creed in church in order to go along with the congregation's corporate worship, even though one, if alone, might be unsure about affirming each individual item thereof."

But we fell apart on our view of the Bible. He could not accept the historic doctrine of its unique divine inspiration, its integrity and authority.

This casual but warm acquaintance flashed through my mind almost 20 years later, when I read that Bishop Pike reported that he had established communication with his dead son Jim.

I suppose my empathy with the Bishop was greater, and certainly my interest in what he reported was increased, by the fact that my own college-student son had also recently died quite suddenly.

Did Bishop Pike really talk with Jim, through mediums?

He certainly thought so, and the movement of objects in the unoccupied flat he had shared with his son in Cambridge, England, the recollection of past events and people through mediums, would seem to support his view. (The full account is found in *The Other Side*, by James A. Pike and Diane Kennedy, Doubleday & Co., Inc., New York.)

The first medium to call up Jim from the dead—and the final one, as related in Dr. Pike's book—was Mrs. Ena Twigg, an Anglican churchwoman who lived in West London. Her word about Jim, or Jim's word through her, was, "I failed the test,

I can't face you, can't face life. I'm confused. Very sudden passing—have had to do this—couldn't find anyone. God, I didn't know what I was doing. But when I got here I found I wasn't such a failure as I thought. My nervous system failed. . . . I'm not in purgatory—but something like hell here. Yet nobody blames me here."

At a later session with Mrs. Twigg, Dr. Pike explored these "brief theological comments," and asked Jim if he had "any new insight."

"Yes," Jim replied (through the medium), "Now I feel there is *Something*. It's beginning to make sense to assume that Someone is making things hang together and develop . . . but since I've been here I haven't heard anything about a Jesus."

Some months later, Mrs. Twigg's trance produced these words from Jim: "This was religion without somebody forcing God and Jesus down my throat. . . . I haven't met [Jesus]. They talk about him—a mystic, a seer, yes, a seer. Oh, but Dad, they don't talk about him as a savior. As an example, you see? . . . Don't you ever believe that God can be personalized. He is the Central Force and you all give your quota toward it. Do you agree with me, Dad?"

Reverend George Daisley, who had come to Santa Barbara, California, from England about five years before, was the next medium with whom Dr. Pike had contact. Edgar Cayce, Dr. Pike's Uncle Bill, his son's maternal grandfather, and Jim himself were raised by Mr. Daisley during his initial seance.

In a later sitting, George Daisley quoted Jim:

"I haven't heard anything personally about Jesus. Nobody around me seems to talk about him. When we come over here, we have a choice: to remain as we are, or to grow in our understanding. Some still seem to be Church-minded and are waiting for a Judgment Day, but these seem to be the unenlightened ones. Others seem to be expanding their mind and self toward more Eastern understandings. I have talked to someone of Chinese origin who offered to help me. He said, 'All of life is a process of evolution and growth.' It seems that the more intellect used, the better—but we're dealing with a 'mind self' which we are fusing with the 'spirit self.' They tell me it will take much endeavor to find the truth.

"A man came to earth who was Jesus, I am sure, and I would assume he came from the sphere where the purified are. I am in the sphere where those who've made mistakes are, but there seems to be no reason why at some period of eternity we can't all be a part of what some call the 'Christ sphere.'"

The other medium through whom Dr. Pike believed he spoke with his son was Reverend Arthur Ford, a Disciples of Christ minister in Philadelphia, Pennsylvania, perhaps the best-known American medium. It was a videotaped seance with Mr. Ford in Toronto, subsequently released on the Canadian Television Network, that alerted the world to Dr. Pike's belief that he had been in communication with his dead son.

In a subsequent seance, Mr. Ford quoted Mrs. Maren Bergrud, Dr. Pike's secretary-assistant (who, after collaborating with him from the beginning of his research into psychic phenomena through mediums, had recently committed suicide) as saying from "the other side": "[Jesus is] just another person, been here longer, but I have been told that the people who have been here long enough to advance to a high plane or a high dimension can always come down to a lower plane to help us. But we who are just here have to earn the right to go up."

10. MRS. TWIGG AND THE WITCH OF ENDOR

WE CAN SAFELY assume that Dr. Pike was neither a bishop thinking theologically, nor a lawyer thinking objectively, but a father in anguish of soul as he visited Mrs. Twigg and the other mediums. And perhaps in the light of all that preceded Jim's suicide, it is not surprising if Dr. Pike desperately wanted reassurance that he was not to blame for the way things had turned out, despite his attempt during several months of living with Jim in Cambridge to redeem his son from the world he had entered through drug addiction. (It must be noted, however, that Dr. Pike denies the need for such reassurance; through his pastoral counseling experience, he says, he had learned to reject simplistic guilt.)

Whether this was so or not, James Pike was never more vulnerable in his life to such an experience, to receive it and believe it, than in the aftermath of Jim's suicide and the later suicide of his close associate, Mrs. Maren Bergrud.

People who visit mediums are almost always emotionally vulnerable. They have not yet come to terms with grief, they often have the ordinary "What if," "Why didn't I," "If only" guilt feelings as they think about the deceased person. And some mediums may pander to such emotional upheaval.

But is it possible to call up the dead? This is the important question.

Since my long-ago conversations with James Pike were in the context of the Bible, I should like to appeal to what it tells us for my answer.

Dead people appeared to living people on two occasions in the Bible, once in the Old Testament and once in the New. One appearance resulted from an appeal to the powers of darkness, and occurred through the activity of a medium. The other was at the time of Jesus' transfiguration, and represented, according to the record, a special act of God.

King Saul was the one who sought out a medium, to consult dead prophet Samuel, in the crisis of imminent attack by the Philistines. His act in consulting the medium was an extreme one: he had previously turned from God; he had been disowned by God; God had refused to answer his request for counsel through ordinary channels and maintained silence.

The extent of King Saul's desperation is shown by the fact that he was willing to take this course, since—in an earlier action as king—he had outlawed mediums and spiritism.

It seems fair to examine this incident in the light of Dr. Pike's experience, since the Bishop himself introduced the comparison in *The Other Side*.

Here's what happened, as it's recorded in I Samuel 28 (*R.S.V.*):

Then Saul said to his servants, "Seek out for

me a woman who is a medium, that I may go to her and inquire of her."

And his servants said to him, "Behold, there is a medium at Endor."

So Saul disguised himself and put on other garments, and went, he and two men with him; and they came to the woman by night. And he said, "Divine for me by a spirit, and bring up for me whomever I shall name to you."

The woman said to him, "Surely you know what Saul has done, how he has cut off the mediums and the wizards from the land. Why then are you laying a snare for my life to bring about my death?"

But Saul swore to her by the Lord, "As the Lord lives, no punishment shall come upon you for this thing."

Then the woman said, "Whom shall I bring up for you?"

He said, "Bring up Samuel for me."

When the woman saw Samuel, she cried out with a loud voice; and the woman said to Saul, "Why have you deceived me? You are Saul."

The king said to her, "Have no fear; what do you see?"

And the woman said to Saul, "I see a god coming up out of the earth."

He said to her, "What is his appearance?"

And she said, "An old man is coming up; and he is wrapped in a robe."

And Saul knew that it was Samuel, and he bowed with his face to the ground and did obeisance.

Then Samuel said to Saul, "Why have you disturbed me by bringing me up?"

Saul answered, "I am in great distress; for the Philistines are warring against me, and God has turned away from me and answers me no more, either by prophets or by dreams; therefore I have summoned you to tell me what I shall do."

And Samuel said, "Why then do you ask me, since the Lord has turned from you and become your enemy? The Lord has done to you as he spoke by me; for the Lord has torn the kingdom out of your hand, and given it to your neighbor, David. Because you did not obey the voice of the Lord, and did not carry out his fierce wrath against Amalek, therefore the Lord has done this to you this day. Moreover the Lord will give Israel also with you into the hand of the Philistines; and tomorrow you and your sons shall be with me; the Lord will give the army of Israel also into the hand of the Philistines."

Then Saul fell at once full length upon the ground, filled with fear because of the words of Samuel; and there was no strength in him, for he had eaten nothing all day and all night. And the woman came to Saul, and when she saw he was terrified, she said to him, "Behold, your handmaid has hearkened to you; I have taken my life in my hand, and have hearkened to what you have said to me. Now therefore, you also hearken to your handmaid; let me set a morsel of bread before you; and eat, that you may have strength when you go on your way."

He refused and said, "I will not eat."

But his servants together with the woman urged him; and he hearkened to their words. So he arose from the earth, and sat upon the bed.

Now the woman had a fatted calf in the house, and she quickly killed it, and she took flour and kneaded it, and baked unleaven bread of it, and put it before Saul and his servants; and they ate. Then they rose and went away that night.

There are several differences between this account and that of Dr. Pike.

First, Saul recognized Samuel. It may have been his voice rather than his appearance, but he didn't have to take the medium's word for it, nor the mention of remote facts or persons for evidence. (Subsequent to the televised seance with Reverend Arthur Ford, some of this surprising "evidence" was shown by *Newsweek* Magazine to have been available in the *International Who's Who*. Dr. Pike mentions this, in admitting a possibility—which he did not accept—that he had been the victim of a hoax or conspiracy on the part of the various mediums.)

Then, too, Samuel talked like Samuel. Here was a dead man, not expressing himself in bits and pieces of obscure phrases and ideas—like most recorded conversations through mediums—but thundering as he had before they laid him in the grave.

The witch did not treat the appearance casually as did the mediums James Pike consulted; nor did she go into a trance. She was terrified. Perhaps her terror was related to fear for her life because she had broken the command of the king

70

standing before her. But it seems to many Old Testament scholars that she was terrified by what she had brought back from the other side.

Like many reported communications through mediums, the word James Pike received denied the biblical concept of God and Jesus Christ. Samuel's word to King Saul, on the other hand, affirmed the personality of the God of Israel, and declared His impending judgment.

The other major biblical occasion on which the dead appeared was when Old Testament prophet-leaders Moses and Elijah, who had died centuries before, appeared on a mountain with Jesus in the presence of three disciples.

And after six days Jesus took with him Peter and James and John his brother, and led them up a high mountain apart. And he was transfigured before them, and his face shone like the sun, and his garments became white as light. And behold, there appeared to them Moses and Elijah, talking with him.

And Peter said to Jesus, "Lord, it is well that we are here; if you wish, I will make three booths here, one for you and one for Moses and one for Elijah."

He was still speaking, when lo, a bright cloud overshadowed them, and a voice from the cloud said, "This is my beloved Son, with whom I am well pleased; listen to him."

When the disciples heard this, they fell on their faces, and were filled with awe.

But Jesus came and touched them, saying, "Rise, and have no fear."

And when they lifted up their eyes, they saw no one but Jesus only.

And as they were coming down the mountain, Jesus commanded them, "Tell no one the vision, until the Son of Man is raised from the dead." (Matthew 17, *R.S.V.*)

Here is no quiet cottage or darkened room, no trance or disembodied voices. This is an appearance outdoors, on a mountain. The dead appear as in life, they talk with a living man, the onlookers —as was true of the incident involving King Saul —are terrified and fall on their faces.

And there is no uncertainty about the nature of God or of Jesus. Unlike Bishop Pike's experience with mediums, the incident is consonant with other biblical teachings. God speaks, and in speaking affirms His Son.

Did Bishop Pike actually get through to his dead son Jim, and to Maren Bergrud, through mediums?

Dr. Pike was convinced that the answer was yes, although he considered at some length the possibility that he had been duped by the mediums he consulted, individually or collectively. He concluded that all had acted in good faith, and had produced words from "the other side." (At times, he thought, they spoke on their own, along the lines of a sympathetic pastoral counselor who presents little thoughts or homilies to an inquirer. He distinguished between these thoughts and true breakthroughs.)

But Pike was a public figure. Research could have uncovered many things about his past that he'd forget had ever been printed or spoken. By his own admission, for instance, he had been on hundreds of television shows.

Was there an interlocking network of mediums —Mrs. Twigg, George Daisley, Arthur Ford—in England and the United States, who conspired to manipulate Bishop Pike—a world figure—for their purposes, without his knowledge? No, says Pike, these were people of probity and integrity. But to those who know the extent to which zealous men will go to achieve their mission (in this case, the advancement of spiritism), his elaborate reasons will be less than convincing.

Still, what comes through has a certain ring of truth to it. All that Bishop Pike heard in the seances may not have come from "the other side," may not have been the words of his son Jim or the other dead people who claimed to speak; but a lot of it seems to have come, at the very least, from beyond the mediums.

Where did it come from?

11. JESUS AND THE UNSEEN WORLD

TWICE IN THE past dozen years I have been brushed by the invisible. I have no other explanation for what happened.

The first time was a fall day in Philadelphia. Mrs. Bayly and I had taken our four-year-old boy to Children's Hospital in center city for the blood tests he had to have every two weeks because he had leukemia. It was an anxious, uncertain two hours before we would receive the report and learn whether the dread disease was still in check or not.

To pass the time, we walked seven or eight blocks to John Wanamaker's department store. As we crossed City Hall courtyard, with Danny between us, we passed a blind girl who was seated there begging for money.

"You don't know whether to give to such a person or not," I said. "You don't really know whether they need it, or how they'll spend it."

"You don't need to know," Mary Lou replied. "Jesus said we should give just because someone asks."

By then we had passed the young woman. We crossed the street to Wanamaker's, where we had lunch and tried to be cheerful.

Afterwards I suggested to Mary Lou that she might window-shop while I walked back to Children's with Danny to get the results. She could meet us later.

So my little boy and I left the store, crossed the street and walked back through City Hall courtyard. Again we passed the beggar girl. This time, remembering Mary Lou's words, I dropped a quarter into her tin cup.

Now remember that she was blind; but even if she wasn't, we were a half-dozen blocks from the hospital and Danny outwardly appeared completely well. And Mary Lou and I had not discussed his sickness or the hospital tests in front of Danny as we walked. We wanted to forget it for two hours.

As I leaned over to drop in my coin, the girl said, "God is able to make your little boy well."

The other time was in Logan International Airport, Boston. I was about to fly back to Philadelphia.

This was during a sort of lean period for us, and through poor planning I was ten cents short of the money I needed to get home.

As I walked into the terminal building, I said within myself, not closing my eyes, "Thank you, God, for ten cents."

A moment later I heard a coin drop to the floor. I didn't look down, or stop, because I knew it wasn't mine. Someone tugged at my sleeve and said, "This belongs to you." And he put a quarter in my hand.

People were going in all directions. Whoever it was disappeared in the crowd.

For a moment I continued to hold my hand outstretched, the coin still in it, so that whoever really owned it could take it from me. Then I said, "Thank you, God, for a quarter," and put it in my pocket.

The second incident represented God's intervention in ordinary life to meet my need. I prayed and He answered.

I'm not so sure about the first. It was an intervention, but I can't be sure of its source: was it the power of God or the power of darkness?

"God is able to make your little boy well" was certainly true. This would lead me to believe that God was responsible for the strange utterance of these words. Yet the words raised my hopes, and after an hour, Mary Lou's when I told her. But four months later Danny died.

I'm not sure that God would raise our hopes only to dash them. Still, He may have affirmed His power to heal to reassure us, when our child's death later came, that it was an act of His will.

There is, of course, another possibility to explain this incident that I don't like to admit, although I must. I could have imagined that the blind girl made the statement; it could have been real in my mind without having any objective reality in fact.

I don't believe this was so, and the fact that I told Mary Lou about the incident and repeated the words to her so soon afterward makes me sure that I had no thought of any possibility of my imagining it at the time. But I am aware of the pressure I was under, and I know the fallibility of the mind, including my own mind.

But there's the problem with a lot of strange

psychic incidents: the human mind cannot be depended on, especially under stress.

Regardless of the explanation of isolated data, I believe that we are not limited to the "real" world we can see; there is an equally real world we cannot see.

That unseen world became highly visible, I believe, when Jesus Christ appeared on planet earth. Some insights into the spirit world are available in the New Testament records of His life.

He affirmed the reality of Satan, the devil, and talked with him. Jesus did not question Satan's power, although He refused personally to yield to it. Instead He affirmed God's supreme power and said God alone should be served.

Jesus also recognized the reality of demons, spirit beings who are subservient to Satan. He delivered men from demonic possession and power, in some cases after years of bondage, outcast by society. On one occasion He gave demons permission at their request to enter a herd of swine. The swine bolted over a cliff into the sea and died.

When Jesus' identity was still hidden from his human contemporaries, and hardly perceived by His close associates, demons knew Him and shouted that He was the Son of God. "Why do you come to trouble us?" they cried. (I am reminded of the obsession the mediums Bishop Pike consulted seemed to be under, or the ones who spoke through them from "the other side," to talk about Jesus.)

Jesus did not talk with dead people through a medium, nor act as a medium. According to the record he raised dead people, brought them back to life from the other side: a man, the only support of his widowed mother, as his dead body was being carried to the cemetery; the daughter of a synagogue ruler, Jairus; a man who had been in the grave four days.

Jesus also prayed to His Father, acknowledged that He was dependent on His power. While He lived on earth, Jesus had an open channel to the unseen world.

He seemed to have powers of extra-sensory perception. He knew what men were thinking; saw Nathanael when he was hidden from view, at a distance, alone; told Peter that he'd find a coin inside a fish he would later catch; knew undisclosed details of a strange woman's personal life; perceived—in a crowd—a woman's touch behind his back, a touch that healed her from a twelve-year illness.

On one occasion, Old Testament prophet-leaders Moses and Elijah appeared on a mountain with Jesus and conversed with Him. This was in the sight and hearing of three of Jesus' disciples. He was glorified, His face became radiant, and His clothing shone as a voice from the sky announced: "This is my beloved Son, in whom I am well pleased; hear Him."

Jesus Christ claimed to be a manifestation of the unseen world to men. "Our eyes saw Him, our ears heard Him, our hands handled Him" was the disciple John's description of the wonder. He was called God-appearing-in-human-flesh.

The day He died, the bodies of many dead men left their tombs and roamed the streets of Jerusalem, appearing to people after His resurrection.

After He was buried, on the third day, Jesus

amazed His followers by appearing to them on a number of different occasions. He ate broiled fish and a piece of honeycomb with them, talked and walked with them.

But He was different somehow from the One they had known before His death. He appeared in a room at a time when the door was shut. His friends were thoroughly frightened. He answered Thomas' doubts by inviting him to touch the nail-prints in His hands, the spear hole in His side.

After 40 days of post-death appearances, He arose into the sky, where a cloud received Him out of His followers' sight.

The battle between two different worlds of the unseen continued in the early church. Stephen cried out with joy at glimpsing the beyond: heaven opened, and Jesus Christ was standing beside the throne of His Father. He was stoned to death. Paul delivered a girl sorceress from her bondage to demonic spirits opposed to God; her owners, who had been exploiting her, raised a tremendous storm of protest against the Apostles; as a result, they were imprisoned. On another occasion, with Barnabas, Paul stood against Elymas, a sorcerer who was trying to undo their work. Elymas was temporarily blinded.

You say these things are myths, incredible stories? Perhaps so, but are they less believable than your horoscope—those words based on the idea that planets and stars in your birthday sky control your destiny today, reveal your future?

Will you believe in Anton LaVey's church of Satan in San Francisco, but ridicule the idea of Satan in Jerusalem at the time of Christ, Satan in

Berlin at the time of Hitler? Will you fear the influence of such a witch as Sybil Leek, or some dark influence in your neighborhood, while ridiculing the idea of demon possession in the New Testament?

And what of believing that James Pike talked with his dead son through a medium? Can you accept this and not believe that the Witch of Endor brought back dead Samuel at King Saul's request?

There is an unseen spirit world.

It is a world that throbs with the presence of God and the influence of Satan.

Satan seeks to bring humans to the conviction that he exists and God doesn't, that his dark power is the only authority underlying individual and corporate human existence and the universe itself. If they're already convinced of the reality of God's existence, and His sovereignty, Satan may try to cover up his own existence, to hide his actions from their view.

But he's here, even though he's as invisible to our eyes as God is. And the climate in which he works, his goals are the opposite of God's: darkness instead of light; lying instead of truth ("The Devil," Jesus said, "was a liar from the beginning"); war instead of peace; fear and violence instead of love.

12. OUR YEARNING FOR MYSTERY

THE TIMES in which we live seem ideal for a renascence of spiritism.

Mass anxiety exists among people of various cultures, social and economic conditions. People are running scared. The older generations feel threatened by the younger, the younger are frustrated and angry. This anger is focused on the dehumanization of life, the bigness of social institutions.

"I am a human being. Do not fold, spindle or mutilate" is a sign often found in campus demonstrations. With these words students protest the ubiquity of computers and I.D. numbers, of mechanical responses to human problems. It's hard to get simple things done, pressures only seem to increase, the future isn't perceived as in any sense bright.

Problems of war, of environmental pollution, of poverty and injustice have people of all ages uptight. But especially the young, who possess the greatest amount of future.

And so people look for a way out. They look inward with psychedelic drugs, music, strobe lights; they look outward to sexual experience, the sort of simplicity represented by communal living.

There's a mystical element to all this. There's an attempt to wash away what can be seen—the machine, the dirt, the fear, the injustice, the uncertainty—with what cannot be seen but can only be felt.

Not felt with the hands, but with the heart; not filling the belly, but touching the spirit, maybe only touching it as with a feather—but touching it.

Another age might have turned to the church with its anxiety and desire for a mystical element in life. But to many people, today's church seems impotent because it is identified with the problems it should be solving. They see the church as a mere authenticator of the American establishment. The individual is a unit to be counted in large church meetings, his money rung up, just as he is counted by business, university and government for their purposes. Real estate is more important than compassion and justice. Spiritual authority is lost in a maze of uncertainty. Dead tradition and erratic change annihilate mystery. Beauty's holiness, or holiness's beauty, fades before pragmatism and expediency.

But the desire for mystery, our hunger for something beyond computers and commuting, will be satisfied: because we're human. I am a human being. I laugh, I weep, I fear, I sit and watch the ocean break on shore under pale moon. I ask whether there is anything beyond ocean and moon, tears and laughter, body and hands.

Perhaps still more, the human bound to sidewalks and garbage, noise and pollution, who never sits by ocean looking across unbroken sky, sees his need, humanity's need, for something beyond.

Astrologers answer those feelings. Mediums respond. For a fee, whether it's paid directly or by paying for the newspaper or magazine that carries a horoscope column.

But don't put them down for this. The psychiatrist also charges a fee. So does the church, or at least it accepts offerings. And what they deliver is often void of mystery.

Anxiety is answered by astrology. Horoscopes may indicate what the stars have dictated for us. If they do, to be forewarned is to be forearmed.

Dark death is penetrated by mediums, or so they claim. A seance opens a door to the beyond and permits a voice to come through, a voice that may tell us what the condition of our loved one is. The voice will not tell us much, but it will vaguely confirm our hope that death is a door rather than a wall. And it will comfort us.

But can we be sure? Can we know that the voice really comes from the other side, that the medium isn't a fake?

And if the medium has actually established communication with the spirit world, can we be sure that the spirits are truthful and not lying? Perhaps the voices from beyond are meant to delude rather than enlighten us.

There's at least a possibility that we are plunging into deeper problems than those we already face when we consult mediums or follow our horoscope.

Eileen J. Garrett is a medium and president of the American Society for Psychical Research. She speaks about America's current obsession with the "shabby trade of the soothsayer" in her book, *The*

Sense and Nonsense of Prophecy. "On the one hand [America] is hardboiled enough to sneer at anything it cannot see or understand. On the other hand, it is gullible enough to patronize the fortune-tellers who infest our cities. It spends large sums of money to hear such astounding revelations as 'You're a good friend but a dangerous enemy' or 'Don't argue with your boss next Wednesday.' People who profess to tell fortunes with spectacular ease often have sensitivity to a marked degree, which they deliberately use and abuse."

Maybe there's a better way.

13. WHO NEEDS HOROSCOPES?

IT IS LATE afternoon of a Midwest winter's day. I write in growing darkness, surrounded and oppressed, at last aware that I can hardly see the tablet on my knees.

Cold night settles round the house and flows into my room. I am part of it, my work must soon end because of dark.

I put my pen down on the raised hearth beside my chair, get up and turn on the light.

There is relief in knowing that I need not stay in winter's dark, that I can by that small act of mine be surrounded with warm brightness.

The outside dark still grows. But in my house, my room, I choose the light.

Our days are winter's twilight of a century long darkening. Four wars, the destroyer Hitler, a bomb from hell have brought their dark. Witches gather, men marvel, "What hath Satan wrought."

I feel the colding dark. I cannot light the closing of a century, but I can bring bright light to my small room. I need not settle for darkening twilight's coming night.

You share my choice, we have it because we're men and God's God.

"I am the light of the world," Jesus said. "The man or woman who follows me shall not walk in darkness, but shall have the light of life."

Satan and witches, hell, demons and ignorance, bondage, dread fear, horoscopes even and Ouija boards, are creatures of the night.

But I need not choose them. I need not fear them.

I can turn on the light in my small room. I can choose the Light of the World.

The switch that brings this light to me is faith, faith that God, by Jesus Christ, can light my dark world. The more helpless I feel at overcoming the darkness, the more likely I am to turn the switch.

And what about the future? Must I listen to Jeane Dixon or some dark medium interpret the pale flicker of distant stars? Is this the light I want?

No; I want God, Creator of stars and constellations and earth and me. But not merely Creator.

"You have a Father," Jesus said. "Your Father made the stars and rules their courses. But He isn't just interested in light years, in distant universes. He's concerned about the very smallest creature, a sparrow that falls to earth in winter.

"If God sees the sparrow, does He not see you? He does, he even knows the number of hairs on your head. Nothing about you is insignificant to your Father.

"So give your attention to God and His kingdom, His righteousness, and He'll take care of the rest. Trust your Father and you'll not need astrologers and sorcerers and Ouija boards."

The Old Testament prophet Isaiah saw this: "And when they say to you, 'Consult the mediums and the wizards who chirp and mutter,' should not a people consult their God? Should they consult the dead on behalf of the living?"

Who needs horoscopes, seances that raise the dead to strange, halting utterances? Those who have no faith in a living God, who have not yet discovered that there's a switch of faith to turn, that they have a Father who wants to flood their lives with light.

"To the teaching and to the testimony! Surely for this word which they speak there is no dawn. They will pass through the land, greatly distressed and hungry; and when they are hungry, they will be enraged and will curse their king and their God, and turn their faces upward; and they will look to the earth, and behold, distress and darkness, the gloom of anguish; and they will be thrust into thick darkness." (Isaiah 8, *R.S.V.*)

The more dark the country around becomes, the more we need our bright room.

This is no time to turn off the lights.

amulet   ornament inscribed with a magic spell or sign, usually worn around the neck or wrist to ward off evil and to help the wearer

animism   belief that inanimate objects, such as rocks, trees, the wind, are alive and have souls

astrology   study of the position of the stars in order to understand and predict their influence on human affairs and world events such as floods, earthquakes, etc.

augury   practice of divination; omen, sign, portent

bewitch   to influence, especially harmfully, by witchcraft; to cast a spell

black magic   witchcraft. Sometimes called black art

charm   act or spell having magic power. Something worn by a person to ward off evil

clairvoyance   ability to discern things that are not yet present to the senses

conjure   to summon a departed spirit or a devil, often by incantation *coven*   an assembly of (thirteen) witches

crystal gazer   person who uses a crystal ball to look into the future

curse   to call harm or injury upon a person; or the injury that comes in response to the invocation

demon   evil attendant power or spirit, subservient to Satan

divination   practice of seeking to foretell or foresee the future and discover hidden knowledge, often by means of omens, augury, or other occult means

exorcism   ritual used to drive away an evil spirit

E.S.P.   abbreviation for extra-sensory perception

extra-sensory perception   ability to gain insights or knowledge without the use of ordinary senses (sight, hearing, smell, etc.)

familiar   spirit embodied in an animal which attends, serves and guards a person

fetish   object regarded as magical or sacred by primitive people, for use in avoiding evil and attracting good for the owner

fortune-teller   one who tells future events, usually for individuals

hex   to affect by an evil spell; or the sign used to ward off evil spirits *horoscope*   diagram showing position of planets and stars with their signs of the zodiac, used by astrologers to foretell events of a person's life and give related guidance

incantation   charm or spell that is spoken or sung as part of a magical ritual.

magic   supernatural power over natural forces, by use of charms, spells, etc. (Not to be confused with sleight-of-hand tricks often performed on stage.)

medium   individual who acts as a means of communication between this world and the spirit world, with ability to talk to and call up the dead

necromancy   conjuring spirits for the purpose of revealing the future or influencing future events

occult   secret, mysterious, relating to supernatural agencies or forces

Ouija board   flat wooden surface with the alphabet and other signs, used to obtain spiritualistic or telepathic messages about the future or other hidden knowledge. This is sometimes considered a game.

palmistry   reading a person's character or future by the lines on his palms

phrenology   reading a person's character or future by the conformation of his skull

poltergeist   noisy, mischievous ghost who is said to be responsible for strange noises such as rappings or knockings, or movement of inanimate objects. Poltergeists seem to be especially ready to perform around young girls.

precognition   discernment about an event not yet experienced, achieved by means beyond the ordinary physical senses

premonition   uneasy anticipation of an event without any conscious reason for anxiety

presentiment   feeling that something is about to happen

psi   generic symbol for the transcendent aspect of human personality. From first letter of Greek word *psyche* (soul)

psychic   person who is sensitive to nonphysical forces and their significance in the material world

psychic phenomena   events that cannot be explained by physical reference, so are attributed to nonphysical or spiritual forces

reincarnation   rebirth of a soul into a new human body or other form of life. An element of the Hindu religion

Satanism   devil worship, usually involving a travesty of Christian rites

seance   group meeting to receive communication from spirits. A medium usually presides at a seance.

seer   one who predicts future events or developments

soothsaying   act of foretelling future events

sorcery   use of power obtained from control of, or the help of, evil spirits, especially for divination or necromancy

spell   spoken word or pattern of words with magical power

spiritism, or *spiritualism*   belief that departed spirits commune with living people, usually through a medium, but sometimes through other psychic phenomena

tarot cards   set of 22 picture playing cards used in fortune-telling

telepathy, or *mental telepathy*   communication from one mind to another without use of the ordinary physical channels of hearing, seeing, touching, etc.

trance   state of partially suspended animation

voodoo   religion derived from African ancestor worship practiced by Negroes of the West Indies, involving spells, necromancy, and communication with animistic gods

warlock   one who works black magic; *obs.* a male witch

witch   woman or man who practices the black arts; one who has supernatural powers because of a pact with the devil

witchcraft   communion with the devil for purposes of working evil

witches' sabbath or *sabbat*   midnight assembly
of coven of witches for performing rites

wizard   skilled magician, sorcerer

zodiac   imaginary belt of planets and constellations in twelve houses which affect human experience, represented by astrological signs

The Bible, especially the records of Jesus' life on earth: Matthew, Mark, Luke, John. *Revised Standard Version* and *Jerusalem Bible* are very readable.

Garrett, Eileen J. *The Sense and Nonsense of Prophecy.* New York: Garrett-Helix, 1969.

Glendenning, O. N. V. *The World of the Witches.* Chicago: University of Chicago Press, 1964.

Koch, Kurt. *Between Christ and Satan.* Baden: Evangelization Publishers, 1967.

————.*Christian Counseling and Occultism.* Grand Rapids: Kregel, 1965.

Lea, Henry C. *Superstition and Force.* Philadelphia: Collins, 1878.

Lewinsohn, Richard. *Prophets and Prediction.* London: Stecker & Warburg, 1958.

M'Donald, W. *Spiritualism.* New York: Carlton and Porter, 1866.

Meerlo, Joost A. M. *Hidden Communion, Studies in the Communication Theory of Telepathy.* New York: Garrett Publications, 1964.

Oesterreich, T. K. *Possession, Demonical and Other.* New York: Richard R. Smith, 1930.

Phillips, J. B. *Ring of Truth.* New York: Macmillan Co., 1967.

Pike, James A., with Kennedy, Diane. *The Other*

Side. Garden City: Doubleday & Co., Inc., 1968.

Proceedings, Society for Psychical Research. London: Kegan, Paul, Trench, Trübner and Co., 1901.

Rhine, J. B. *Extra-Sensory Perception.* Boston: Bruce Humphries, 1935.

Upham, Charles W. *Salem Witchcraft.* Boston: Wiggin & Lunt, 1867.

Williams, Charles, *Witchcraft.* Cleveland: World Publishing Co., 1959.